Taylor Lautner

by Sheila Griffin Llanas

☆ ☆ ☆ ☆

CAPSTONE PRESS
a capstone imprint

Snap Books are published by Capstone Press,
151 Good Counsel Drive, P.O. Box 669, Mankato, Minnesota 56002.
www.capstonepub.com

Printed in the United States of America in North Mankato, Minnesota.
032010
005740CGF10

Books published by Capstone Press are manufactured with paper
containing at least 10 percent post-consumer waste.

Library of Congress Cataloging-in-Publication Data
Llanas, Sheila, 1944–
    Taylor Lautner / by Sheila Griffin Llanas.
        p. cm.
    Includes bibliographical references and index.
    Summary: "Describes the life and career of Taylor Lautner"—Provided by publisher.
    ISBN 978-1-4296-4999-5 (library binding.)
    1. Lautner, Taylor, 1992—Juvenile literature. 2. Actors—United States—Biography—Juvenile literature.
I. Title.

PN2287.L2855G75 2011
791.4302'8092—dc22
    [B]   2010004483

Editor: Mari Bolte
Designer: Juliette Peters
Media Researcher: Marcie Spence
Production Specialist: Laura Manthe

Photo Credits:
AP Images/Dana Edelson/NBCU Photobank, 27; AP Images/Vince Bucci/PictureGroup, cover; Alamy/Photos 12, 12;
DZilla/BauerGriffin, 5; Capital Pictures, 23; Getty Images Inc./Brad Barket, 17; Getty Images Inc./Jeffrey Mayer/
WireImage, 29; Getty Images Inc./Vince Bucci, 18; Globe Photos/Nina Prommer, 13; Johnstone/Raishbrook/Splash News,
7; Newscom, 20, 21, 28; Newscom/Imprint Entertainment/Maverick Films/Summit Entertainment, 16; Newscom/Summit
Entertainment, 24; Newscom/UPI Photo/Keizo Mori, 25; Rex USA/Jim Smeal/BEImages, 10; Rex USA/Picture Perfect,
15; SportMartialArts.com, 9.

Essential content terms are **bold** and are defined at the bottom of the page where they first appear.

Table of Contents

Taylor Hits High Speeds

Taylor Lautner revved the engine of his dirt bike. His muscles rippled under a black T-shirt and dark-wash jeans. A leather jacket completed his look. A pale girl with dark brown hair jumped on the back of the bike. The pair sped away from Forks High School.

Of course, this wasn't real life. Taylor was on a movie **set** in Vancouver, British Columbia, Canada. He was in character as Jacob Black. Taylor and his costars were busy shooting an action scene for *Eclipse*, the third movie in the *Twilight* saga.

Although he practiced hard, Taylor was nervous about shooting the dirt bike scene in *Eclipse*. He only got two takes to get it right!

set—the scenery for a play or movie

Before filming *Eclipse*, Taylor had never driven a dirt bike. He took lessons and practiced for two days. He wanted to prove that he could do his own stunt riding. He was disappointed that the best action scenes were **CGI**—especially the parts where Jacob transforms to a wolf. Taylor didn't want a stunt double to stand in for any of Jacob's human scenes.

Riding a dirt bike wasn't Taylor's only stunt. During another rehearsal, he carried costar Kristen Stewart in his arms for hours in pouring rain. And, of course, there was the clash between Jacob and Edward, the vampire played by Robert Pattinson. Through it all, Taylor didn't complain. Dangerous stunts, bad weather, and romance are just part of his job.

"The physical side was really fun. Some of it was challenging. I've never ridden a dirt bike before and yes, I rode the dirt bike for a total of five seconds in the film. But for those five seconds, I had to look as cool as possible. So it did require a lot of practice just for safety wise so they could let me do it."

—Taylor on doing the stunts for *Eclipse* in an interview with ComingSoon.net.

CGI—moving images created by computer; CGI stands for computer generated images

Taylor showed off his football moves during a photo shoot for *Rolling Stone* magazine.

Taylor the Athlete

Taylor is a natural athlete, excelling in karate, football, and baseball. He played running back and middle linebacker for the Castaic Cougars, his high school football team. In the William S. Hart Baseball Program, he played center field and second base. Taylor's athletic ability translates well to the dance floor too. He has performed hip-hop dance with LA Hip Kids and jazz dance with Hot Shots.

A Karate Kid

This rising Hollywood star was born into an average family. Taylor Daniel Lautner was born February 11, 1992, in Grand Rapids, Michigan. His mom, Deborah, is a software developer. His dad, Daniel, works as an airline pilot.

When Taylor was 4, a fire burned down the family house when they were away. The Lautners settled into a new house in Hudsonville, Michigan. Taylor was 6 when his little sister, Makena, was born. A Maltese dog named Roxy completed the family.

Just after starting school at Jamestown Elementary in Hudsonville, 6-year-old Taylor became interested in karate. He was a natural at flips and tricks. After only a year, Taylor won his first national tournament. At the tournament, he met world champion karate instructor Mike Chat, who would become his trainer. At age 8, Taylor earned the title of Junior World Forms and Weapons Champion. He competed in karate for the next several years.

Taylor was one of the first members of the martial arts group XMA Performance Team.

Hollywood loved watching Taylor in action. He showed off his skills in movies, on the red carpet, and on the show *America's Most Talented Kids*.

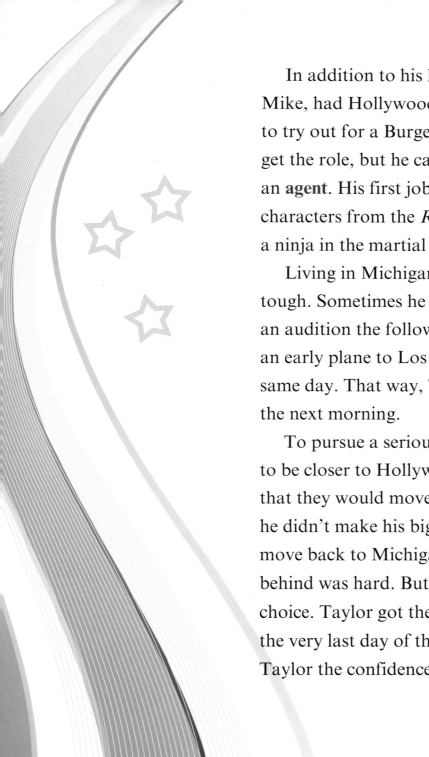

In addition to his karate knowledge, Taylor's coach, Mike, had Hollywood connections. He urged Taylor to try out for a Burger King commercial. Taylor didn't get the role, but he caught the acting bug. He also got an **agent**. His first job was for a commercial featuring characters from the *Rugrats* cartoon. In 2001 he played a ninja in the martial arts movie *Shadow Fury*.

Living in Michigan made Taylor's daily schedule tough. Sometimes he would get a late night call for an audition the following day. The family would take an early plane to Los Angeles and fly back late on the same day. That way, Taylor could still get to school the next morning.

To pursue a serious career in acting, Taylor needed to be closer to Hollywood. Taylor's parents told him that they would move to Los Angeles for a month. If he didn't make his big break after 30 days, they would move back to Michigan. Leaving friends and family behind was hard. But the move proved to be a good choice. Taylor got the callback he was waiting for—on the very last day of the trial month. That callback gave Taylor the confidence to continue acting.

agent—someone who helps actors find work

Steady Acting Work

In Hollywood, Taylor won small roles on TV shows. He also did voice-over work on cartoons like *What's New, Scooby Doo?* and *Duck Dodgers.* But Taylor wanted to do more than be on TV. He wanted to be a movie star.

In 2005 Taylor tried out for the 3D movie *The Adventures of Sharkboy and Lavagirl.* Taylor showed the director, Robert Rodriguez, his martial arts moves. Even though Rodriguez chose Taylor right away, he made Taylor wait a month to learn he got the part.

Taylor played Sharkboy, a superhero who was raised by sharks. Taylor was on-set for three months in Austin, Texas. Taylor studied hard to keep up with his school work. But it was worth it. He got to do all his own stunts. He even got to **choreograph** some scenes.

Playing a superhero was a new experience for Taylor.

choreograph—to design or plan the movements of a dance or other display

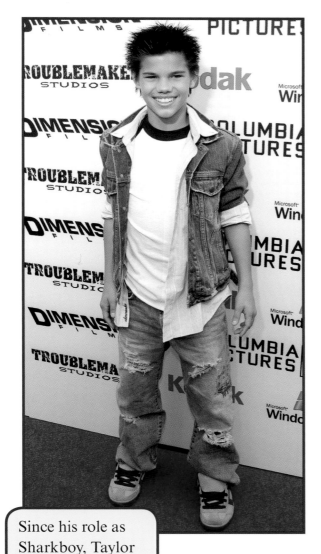

Since his role as Sharkboy, Taylor has been a favorite with the press.

The movie premiered in Los Angeles on June 4, 2005. Taylor, then age 13, showed up in a denim jacket, ripped jeans, and unlaced shoes. He did more than pose on the red carpet. He pulled off acrobatic flips and leaps. The press loved it.

Playing Sharkboy even won Taylor some fans. "I'd be in the store, and boys would whisper to their moms," Lautner told *People* magazine in an interview. "Then the moms would say, 'Excuse me, are you Sharkboy?'"

Taylor didn't get star treatment at home. He was a straight-A student at Valencia High School in Santa Clarita. His parents asked him to do chores, and they gave him an allowance. Taylor still did normal kid things. He loved watching the movie *The Last Samurai* and eating his favorite dinner, steak with A-1 sauce. Cake batter ice cream was the perfect way to end the day.

In 2005 Taylor got a small part in the movie *Cheaper by the Dozen 2*. The next year, he got a role on the show *Love, Inc.* He also did some more voice-over work. In 2008 he appeared in the TV show *My Own Worst Enemy* as the son of star Christian Slater. Those were Taylor's last bit parts. Taylor was about to transform from an unknown actor to a huge star.

Twilight Approaches

In late 2007, filmmakers began their search for actors to appear in the movie based on the popular book *Twilight*. In January 2008, an **open casting call** was held in Portland, Oregon. Teen boys tried out for the small role of Jacob Black, a friend of the main character, Bella Swan. Taylor hadn't even heard of the *Twilight* books. But his agent told him to give it a shot.

Taylor showed up early for his audition. He read lines with Kristen Stewart, who had already been cast as Bella. They read from the script and acted out scenes from *New Moon* and *Eclipse*.

A month later, Taylor got a call. His dad, agent, and manager were all listening in. Together they learned that Taylor had earned the part of Jacob Black. At 16, he would be *Twilight's* youngest star.

open casting call—an audition where anyone is allowed to try out

Hundreds of fans greeted Taylor at Mann's Village Theatre before the *Twilight* premiere.

Prepping for the Role

Taylor read *Twilight*, but not the rest of the books. He didn't want to know how Jacob changed. Eventually, he did read all four books. In the series, Jacob is a member of the Quileute tribe. Taylor learned the American Indian tribe's legends and met some tribal members. He even learned to speak a little of their language.

Around the same time, Taylor decided that his career was causing him to miss too much school. He tested out of high school and began taking college courses. But he did go to his high school prom, taking a friend as his date. And he made his first big purchase with his paycheck—a Mac Powerbook.

Taylor and his on-screen dad, Gil Birmingham (seated), had an instant connection.

Stephenie Meyer wrote *Twilight* in three months. *New Moon*, *Eclipse*, and *Breaking Dawn* soon followed.

The Origins of Jacob Black

Originally, author Stephenie Meyer created the character of Jacob Black to be Bella's friend in *Twilight*. His role was to help Bella learn Edward's secret. But he was given a bigger part in *New Moon*. "From the very beginning, even when Jacob only appeared in chapter six of *Twilight*, he was so *alive*," Meyer wrote on her Web site. "I couldn't keep him locked inside a tiny role."

Teen girls swooned over Taylor as Jacob Black.

jacob
twilight

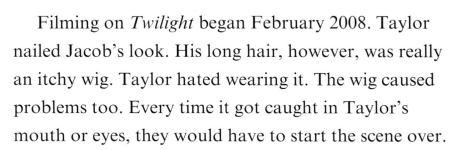

Filming on *Twilight* began February 2008. Taylor nailed Jacob's look. His long hair, however, was really an itchy wig. Taylor hated wearing it. The wig caused problems too. Every time it got caught in Taylor's mouth or eyes, they would have to start the scene over.

The weather was also terrible. Freezing rain and fierce winds made outdoor scenes unbearable. The movie had many tests for Taylor to overcome.

One thing Taylor had to get used to was the instant fame. He didn't realize that Jacob already had a huge following. In August, he was visiting family in Michigan. He dropped in at the local Barnes and Noble store. Nobody knew he would be there. He didn't even tell his agent that he planned on going.

The store was hosting a midnight release party for the final book in the *Twilight* series, *Breaking Dawn*. More than 1,000 girls flocked to the store to get a glimpse of Jacob Black. Taylor stayed until 2:00 a.m., signing autographs and posing for pictures. He wanted to make sure no girl left unhappy.

> " ... I'd look at myself in the mirror and I wouldn't even be able to recognize myself. It was so weird just to see that hair on me. ... it was very itchy, hot, whatever, annoying."
> —Taylor on wearing a wig, from a Fancast.com interview.

Twilight Premiere

When filming wrapped, Taylor and the cast visited six cities in as many days to promote the movie. Thousands of fans showed up at every stop. *Twilight* premiered on November 18, 2008. Taylor did a radio interview with Ryan Seacrest. He greeted fans at the Hot Topic at the Hollywood & Highland Center in Los Angeles. Finally, he walked the red carpet in a black Jean Paul Gaultier suit and open-collar white shirt. He posed for photos with his costars. The movie was a success. It brought $70 million in ticket sales its first weekend.

Taylor signs many autographs for fans.

Taylor and Kristen had no problem portraying the chemistry between Jacob and Bella in *New Moon*.

New Moon Rises

Robert and Kristen were signed immediately to the sequel. To his shock, Taylor was not. Jacob makes a lot of changes in *New Moon*. He goes from a skinny, carefree boy to a huge, muscled werewolf with adult problems. Producers were not convinced Taylor could show Jacob's physical and mental changes.

Taylor knew he could do it, and he fought for the part. The day *Twilight* wrapped, he hired a trainer. He started working out and soon gained 30 pounds of lean muscle. His shirt size went from men's small to a large. A new screen test with Kristen proved they had chemistry. The producers were sold. Taylor had won back his role.

CHAPTER 4

Lights on Taylor

New Moon started filming March 2009. The weather was even worse than it had been during *Twilight*. Taylor did almost all his own stunts. He jumped out of a window, climbed a house, and leaped across fields. But there was one upside. His wig was better!

Team Taylor

In *New Moon*, Bella has to choose between Jacob and Edward. So do *Twilight* fans. "Twihards" took sides, joining either "Team Edward" or "Team Jacob." Taylor was Team Jacob all the way. Taylor's role in *New Moon* even changed the minds of some Team Edward fans.

Taylor explained how to choose your *Twilight* "team" to MTV.—

"[If] you develop this deep friendship and then all of a sudden fall in love later on, then you should be Team Jacob. Come to the dark side. But if you believe in love at first site and seeing that mysterious man in the corner, then all right, join Team Edward."

the twilight saga
new moon
)
11.20.09

Still, it was weird for Taylor to see T-shirts, hats, and underwear printed with Team Jacob and Team Taylor. One fan even asked Taylor to growl like a werewolf. He did it once, but he vowed never to do it again.

Taylor loved the physical aspect of his new role. But it came with a price. The press followed him everywhere. "Honestly, I try and stay away from what's been written about me, because if you let that stuff get to you, and when it's not true, it can drive you crazy," Taylor said in an interview with MoviesOnline.com. To get away from the attention while filming *New Moon*, he hid out at a senior-citizen bowling alley!

Fans debated online for months whether Jacob and Bella would kiss in *New Moon*.

The cast did a nonstop press tour to promote *New Moon*. Taylor flew to Mexico, South America, and Europe. The movie premiered in Los Angeles on November 16, 2009. Taylor wore a dark blue Calvin Klein suit with a gray shirt and a silver skinny tie. More than 3,000 fans chanted his name as he walked the red carpet.

Three days later, Taylor walked the red carpet again, this time in New York City. He wore a Dolce and Gabbana suit, with a striped shirt and silver tie. After the film's screening, limos drove the cast to an exclusive party. The decorations looked like the set of Forks, Washington, complete with a tent, evergreens, and two real timber wolves.

Fans waited outside theaters for days to catch the midnight showing of *New Moon*. Some Twihards bought their tickets online more than two months in advance. More than 2,000 showings sold out before the film was even released. The movie broke opening-day box office records, earning $72 million in ticket sales.

Even before the release of *New Moon*, the actors were working hard on *Eclipse*. This time there was no question of who would play Jacob. *Eclipse* has more fighting, more action, more humor, and more romance. It was Taylor's favorite book of the series.

Taylor flew to Paris, London, and Tokyo to attend premieres of *New Moon*.

What's Next

After a short eight-week break from filming *New Moon*, the cast reunited in Vancouver. They were ready to film the third *Twilight* movie. Filming for *Eclipse* began August of 2009.

Filming wrapped in late October. The cast and crew celebrated with a party at the Vancouver Aquarium. With filming done, Taylor had time to take on a few more jobs.

Taylor's stardom had reached a mega-watt status. His face appeared on magazine racks across the country. In December 2009, he hosted an episode of *Saturday Night Live*.

"I'm having the time of my life, so it couldn't be a better end to my teenage years. I'm doing what I love and I'm spending time with the people I love. So it's great. I'm definitely never, ever going to forget this."

—Taylor, on filming the *Twilight* series, in an interview with *Parade* magazine.

Taylor played a football player, a pop choir member, and a Team Edward fan on *Saturday Night Live*.

In public, Taylor is polite, friendly, and mature. He has an easy time speaking with reporters. His warm attitude has earned him the admiration of the public. No matter how famous he gets, he still acts like an everyday teen. He still gets an allowance. And he has to check in with his on-set **chaperone**—his dad!

Taylor and his father, Daniel, have also entered the entertainment world as producers. Tailor Made Entertainment's first project will be *Cancun*, an action movie starring Taylor.

chaperone—a person who accompanies a younger person in public

In July 2009, Taylor had a break between films. Instead of relaxing, he took a role in the romantic comedy *Valentine's Day*, which opened on its namesake day in 2010. It made more than $52 million and was number one at the box office that weekend. As for the holiday, Taylor loves Valentine's Day. He buys roses for the women in his life and even makes his own cards!

Although his family now lives in Hollywood, Taylor still has ties in Michigan. He goes Jet Skiing, fishing, and trapshooting with his family. Taylor loves to watch college football. His favorite team is the Michigan Wolverines. And he still spends time with his parents. On his 18th birthday, Taylor had a low-key day with friends and family.

When Taylor's at home, he likes eating pizza or Chinese food. He watches *American Idol* and *So You Think You Can Dance?* He's also a big movie fan. He is not ashamed to say he likes romantic movies like *The Notebook* and *Enchanted.* But action movies are his favorite. He loves the *Bourne Identity* series, *Braveheart*, and *Iron Man*.

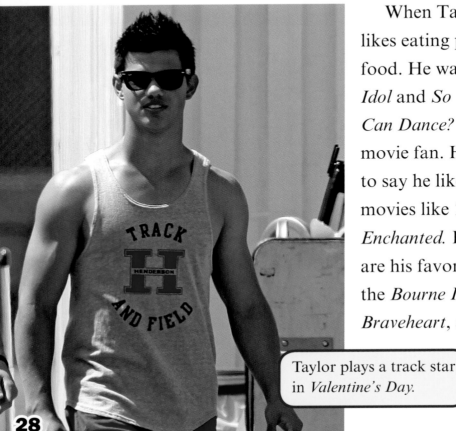

Taylor plays a track star in *Valentine's Day.*

Taylor has a bright future ahead of him as an actor, a director, a producer, or a personal trainer.

Taylor may get the chance to become his own action star. In February 2010, it was announced that Taylor would star in the movie *Stretch Armstrong*. Playing the flexible superhero landed him a $7.5 million paycheck. Taylor's high fees made him the highest-paid teen in Hollywood.

Taylor will also star in the spy-action flick *Abduction*. Along with filming *Breaking Dawn*, Taylor is one busy guy. One day, he might even direct or write. Taylor has so many skills, whatever he chooses next is sure to be a big success!

Glossary

agent (AY-juhnt)—someone who helps actors find work

audition (aw-DI-shuhn)—a tryout performance for an actor

CGI (SEE-GEE-EYE)—moving images created by computer; CGI stands for computer generated images

chaperone (SHAP-uh-rone)—a person who accompanies a younger person in public

choreograph (KOR-ee-oh-graf)—to design or plan the movements of a dance or other display

episode (EP-uh-sode)—one of the programs in a TV or radio series

open casting call (OH-pun KAST-ing CALL)—an audition where anyone is allowed to try out

rehearsal (ri-HURSS-uhl)—a practice performance

set (SET)—the stage or scenery for a play or movie

stunt double (STUNT DUH-buhl)—someone who performs action scenes in place of an actor

take (TAKE)—a filmed scene

voice-over (VOYCE OH-vuhr)—the voice of an animated or offscreen character

Read More

Murphy, Maggie. *Taylor Lautner: Twilight Star.* Young and Famous. New York: PowerKids Press, 2011.

Ryals, Lexi. *Taylor Lautner, Breaking Star: An Unauthorized Biography.* New York: Price Stern Sloan, 2009.

Williams, Mel. *Taylor Lautner.* New York: Simon Pulse, 2009.

Internet Sites

FactHound offers a safe, fun way to find Internet sites related to this book. All of the sites on FactHound have been researched by our staff.

Here's all you do:

Visit *www.facthound.com*

FactHound will fetch the best sites for you!

Index